A *Life's* Journey
in Prose, Songs and Short Stories

John V. Spillman

authorHOUSE®

AuthorHouse™
1663 Liberty Drive
Bloomington, IN 47403
www.authorhouse.com
Phone: 1 (800) 839-8640

Published by AuthorHouse   11/21/2016

ISBN: 978-1-5246-5070-4 (sc)
ISBN: 978-1-5246-5069-8 (e)

Contents

Poems

Song Lyrics

Short Stories

Conclusion

Oh that my words were now written!
oh that they were printed in a book!

Job 19:23

Introduction

You will share the laughter at the ridiculous and cry with the tragedies and relate to each in turn as you take a journey through the rich tapestry of life woven into the prose, songs and short stories that break from the traditional chronological order and instead focus on feelings, emotions and thoughts laid bare over a lifetime and beyond.

John V. Spillman

Poems

Letters

A letter came for us today,
It came from overseas.
It was from our Navy Boy,
We were happy and relieved.

As we read the letter,
Tears came to our eyes,
The letter starts "Dear Mom and Dad,"
A good man often dies.

We were ambushed once today,
We did all that we could.
I hope that you will understand,
I know—I'm sure you would.

I am on the mainland,
In a POW camp.
I am writing slowly,
By a flickering charcoal lamp.

The place I'm in is ugly,
It's dirty and its cold.
I know that I'll be back home again,
I hope, before I'm old.

Although its very cold in here,
And there's very little food,
My mission here is only started,
So far its turned out good.

The Lord will see me through my plight,
He'll never let me down.
He'll guide me through the path of life,
And reward me with a crown.

Remember the age-old saying,
As I'm sure you will,
It's about a poor lost sailor,
That's been "through the mill",

You know you needn't worry,
The Lord is on my side.
And when the end—it's sure to come,
By His side I'll ride.

The only thing that makes me sad,
Is writing this to you.
There is nothing you can say,
But pray—that you can do.

The letter simply ended,
Without a joke or pun.
It was simply stated -
Love Always, from your son.

Now the years have come and gone,
And we are old and gray.
Another letter came today,
It's from our son, we pray.

The letter was from Uncle Sam,
With good word about our boy.
It simply states that he is well,
And serving God with joy.

Another year slipped slowly by,
And everything is still.
Our son is coming back to us,
We pray to God he will.

Our son came back that very day,
And also with his wife.
They both serve God—I know that now,
Through the Christian way of life.

Searching For Peace

The wave of humanity
Is all around,
Yet the city seems deserted.
The traffic noises -
The blaring music -
A solitary being in a sea of humanity.
You wonder what's in life,
The search is not yet over,
You're still not satisfied.
The unknown you are searching for,
Cannot be defined.
The search will yet continue,
Till that certain thing is found,
But where do you look?
In a book that's hard back bound?
There's no set place to look or definition plain.
If its peace you're looking for,
There's one place it is found.
It's found in books with soft-backed,
And also in ones with hard-back bound.
You're wondering where this book is at?
Look not very far
For its as near as your church.
The name of this wonderful book,
Is the Holy Bible friend.

What A Friend Is For

When you're lonely and down on your luck,
With seemingly no one to turn to.
When life becomes a lot of trouble,
And no answer in immediate view.

Do you search and search
and are unable to find,
Someone to tell your sorrows to,
And find that peace of mind?

You're not alone, there's always
Someone That will listen.
Just find a friend, and you will soon
Find the link that's missing.

Your troubles and woes,
You'll find with pleasure,
Will seemingly disappear -
When you talk to a friend.

About them, you see, he does care,
The ending of this tale is Very simple, see—
To find a friend who cares,
And you'll be put at your ease.

Hollywood

Hollywood is a city,
Full of movie stars and fame,
But, Hollywood is also
Full of broken hearts and shame.

It seems to be a perfect place,
To a small-town girl like you,
But, don't let the cover fool you,
It's not good for you to do.

If you were here and mixing in,
It's as plain as it can be,
You'd get hooked on bennies,
Or maybe L.S.D.

Its safer just to stay away,
And save your health for me.
Because I think I love you,
But afraid for it to be.

So, stay there in your small-town home,
And live with what you've got.
For Hollywood is not for you,
A movie star you're not.

Helplessness

When your love— so freely given,
Is long unreturned,
When you still feel the same.
The shock of ultimate separation,
Is almost more than one can bear.
If not for friends and relatives,
While your devotion, not unnoticed
Burns low within your mate.
The hurt you feel and loss you take,
Can't return your slowly—dying love;
You grow more distant and have more woes;
And no one but friends and relatives,
To help to ease the pain.
The deep pain, inflicted in divorce upon a person,
Values begin dwindling to an all-time low.
To find yourself so suddenly alone
and in need of comfort,
Found only now in friends.
Where once your mate, you loved so selflessly,
And never treated wrong;
Left and took her love and everything you own.
Just to add a note of cheer to this saddened state,
Marriage is good– for the right two mates.

Daily Routine

Nothing at all to do each day,
But sweep and clean up floors;
Dumping trash; emptying pails;
Opening and closing doors.

First sweep the floor with giant broom,
And deposit dirt somewhere;
Grab a mop and do not stop
Boring, but not rare.

Sweeping, motion—co-ordination,
Next, we wax the floor;
Let it dry, and then you buff it,
It surely is a bore.

Rinse your mop and dump the pail,
Take your mop out back,
You dance around the building,
In the corner is a rack.

While this is all you do each day,
And when it's three PM;
You shower and think of
Where you could have been.

Money

The root of evil is money,
I guess that's everyone's view.
Without money, I guess we're lonely,
Without it, I guess we're blue.

Stop and think a moment,
On how this world would be,
If money was non-existent,
And all our needs were free.

Money can't buy you happiness,
Money can't buy you peace.
But with it, you can buy a house,
Or you can buy a lease.

Money is used for bribery,
It's used for trade, that's true.
It's used to pay off gangsters,
And used for murder, too.

People kill for money,
People die in vain.
The reasons are so varied,
That is very plain.

Why can't we live in harmony,
And live with what we've got?
Why try and beat the Jones'es,
And be someone we're not?

Until we learn to get along,
And live with what we've got,
And stop those money-hungry murders,
It'll help the world a lot.

And so I add a word or two,
About the present situation.
Murders will be continued,
And bring with it Damnation.

War in Vietnam

The war in Vietnam
Is just a façade and a farce,
So all the other smaller nations say,
When the strongest nation in the world
Is losing men each day.
With so much force– with bad control -
They're fighting without reason.
Politicians say, "Support the war!"
But they know it's not the season.
They want the war to carry on
To jack the taxes high.
So little effort– with little care,
They send our men to die.
Aboard the ships and on the land,
You hear the G. I.'s cry-
"Our mission's not to question why,
Just to do or sometimes die."
Will the politicians get together
And sign some sort of truce?
Or will they sit and calmly watch
Their war become a ruse?
Taxpayers can form the answers,
Its as plain as it can be;
So urge for all-out effort
And the end you will foresee.

I Was There

To our neighbor distant,
The info we passed through.
As we glided softly,
Quiet as the dew.

We knew that danger was at hand,
Just around the corner.
The flash of bombs, the roar of guns,
And then—a silent mourner.

The Captain broke the silence,
By shouting "Full Ahead!"
Next he shouted "Full right rudder"
And then away we sped.

Now the guns are silent,
Just why we do not know.
The only thing we know for sure,
Is that we're riding low.

With the DC party summoned -
Fire party standing by -
The crew, we sat and waited -
The time, it did not fly.

We were at General Quarters,
We knew it would not last.
Then came the word "Abandon ship!
Because we're sinking fast"

Two hundred men, they hit the drink,
And quickly got away.
It still remains a mystery,
Even to this day.

The ship went down in Tonkin Gulf,
And the crew was saved I pray.
You wonder why that I'm so sure,
Because I was there that day.

The Trip

Arise and listen faithful friend,
To this yarn I'm spinning.
Don't get too discouraged,
This is the beginning.

It begins with 'Once Upon a time'
And goes through to the end.
It's a very funny yarn,
The truth I hope will bend.

The star of this hilarity,
They're called 'three musketeers'.
They're a very close-knit group,
They rate their share of cheers.

They began their travels,
With food so very sparse.
Two loaves of bread, a dozen rolls,
And butter– tis no farce.

They began in Long Beach,
One foggy, frozen night.
And were on their way eastbound,
By the time it was daylight.

Their cash reserves were scanty,
Only two dollars ninety-two.
But they had a destination,
And knew just what to do.

It took only half a fortnight,
To come to journey's end.
The joys and pain they suffered,
Became one harmonious blend.

Their return trips were varied,
As you can probably gather.
They came back by plane and bus,
Recurrence? "No," their parents added.

Trip to Vietnam

Today I went to Vietnam,
A friend of mine came too.
We both had the morning watch,
Among the morning dew.

It was so very quiet,
Too quiet– that I know,
A shot rang out– a stifled cry-
My friend was lying low.

I jumped to hide from cover,
A shell was marked for me.
I glanced around the bushes,
But nothing I could see.

The VC I knew were out there,
I could feel it in the air,
My friend was wounded badly,
I know, but had no care.

I had to help that friend of mine,
To sound the battle call.
To my dismay, I could not help -
I could not help at all.

The battle Sargent heard the shot,
And made the battle cry.
My friend was very badly hurt,
I thought that he may die.

The sergeant said, "Don't worry boy,
Help is near at hand."
All the troops we guarded then,
Rushed and formed a band.

We won the fight that morning,
My friend will live I pray,
The doc, he came and told me,
That he would be okay.

A Private War

Somewhere on the west coast,
Is a man called 'Big Bad John'.
And this is his story,
Of how his war he won.

His war was not fought with handguns,
Or mortar shells do big.
His war was fought with emotions,
And not with Russian MIG's.

The battle scene took place I hear,
Aboard a Navy boat.
When his girl, she came to see him,
He called her an old goat.

He and she went round and round,
And never got no place.
If you cold have heard them,
You'd swear there was a race.

The battle lasted briefly,
It was over soon.
And Big Bad John had won again,
He had no cause to moon.

Although he lost the battle,
And won the war they say.
He isn't very happy now,
For his love had left that day.

He couldn't think of what to do,
Or even what to say.
He went to talk to his best friend -
He went to talk to Ray.

They talked for o'er an hour,
When they were finally through.
He seemed to be much happier,
For Ray knew what to do.

And now the scene is closing,
With just a word or two.
When you enter battle—
Find out what to do.

The Sun Forgot to Shine

Today the sun forgot to shine,
Upon the lonely earth,
Tonight the moon is not around,
To shine upon my berth.

As I sit and wonder why,
I ask myself in vain—
Why the sun forgot to shine,
And why it has to rain?

It rains by night and rains by day,
The sun, it shines not through.
The rain clings closely to the ground,
And forms the lonely dew.

The joy of God is in my heart,
His word my mouth does spread.
I do not read the "Book of Life",
I only need to look.

But look I should, and look I don't,
At our God's precious word.
God's word is everlasting,
Not like a mockingbird.

As I looked upon the Word of God,
A miracle occurred.
God's word was like a snow-white dove,
Not like a mockingbird.

Today the sun began to shine,
To fill the earth with joy.
Tonight the moon came back to me,
As if I were still a boy.

God's love I know is in my heart,
His word my mouth does spread.
Of joys untold—of wealth en mass—
I'll spread until I'm dead.

Although I will not be around,
To continue in God's ways.
His Word won't pass away I know,
It'll live past judgment day.

Why Is There A War

The sounds of guns a-roaring,
The shrapnel maim and mar.
You hear the obvious question asked,
Why is there a war?

Help is near from ships afloat,
The Army's on the shore.
Marines safeguarding the entire beach,
Its surely not a bore.

Sweethearts waiting back at home,
Worried folks and wives.
But their fears are all confirmed-
Their beloved, yes, they died.

Tears are shed and the years go on,
The shrapnel continue to maim and mar.
Again, you hear the question asked,
"Why is there a war?"

The soldiers come back home at last,
The war is finally done.
The sweethearts and wives are glad to see,
Their men—the war they won.

But wars are still not over,
Another's raging, yes;
A vigil of waiting for their love,
And to try settling the mess.

The war is not yet over,
And a lot of men were lost.
The President is worried now,
This war will really cost.

More lives are lost each day, I know,
And runs the total high;
The soldiers don't ask the question why,
They just do and sometimes die.

The guns are not yet silent,
The shrapnel maim and mar.
You hear the people always ask,
"Why is there a war?"

Twus da Niet b4 Crismus

Twus da niet b4 Crismus an all tru da pad,
Not a cretur wuz stirn not eevn ol dad.
Da stokkns wur lyn all ovr da floor,
Hopin dat Santa cud find em wunc moor.

Da rugrats wur scattrd all ovr da bed,
Wit vizons of piep smoek curld tru dere hed.
Ma wit er hash piep an me wit a joint,
Wuz crashd on da floor, makin a point.

Win out on da siedwak dere wuz such a clatr,
I stumbld an fell, swarn whut wuz da matr?
Awae 2 da wndr I stumbld an fell,
Peerd out da crakd wndr an sed wha da hell!

Da eree flickr frum da street liet belo,
Gaev da cluttrd yard a sikadelic glo.
An whut wit mi bludshot i's did I spy,
A tinee slay and raendere so hi.

Wit a litl ole drivr so drunkn an sousd,
I new n a moment it wuznt a mous.
Moor crookd din toun drunks his corsrs dey caem,
He chortld an fartd, an slurrd em by naem.

Now cashr, now dancn, now prancn an vixel,
On coopid, on coomit, uh u no da drill.
2 da top o da porch, 2 da top o da wall,
Now go a wae, dat a awae, dat a wae all!

As joints b4 da kitchn mach dey duz liet,
Win dey meet wit de flaem, liets up de niet.
So, up 2 da ruftop dey stumbld an fell,
Wit a slay full o toys an a drunkn ol elf.

An din n a minit I herd on de ruuf,
Da slipn an stumln o each drunkn huuf.
I pulld mi hed n an startd sippn a bud,
Doun da chimlee da drunk elf caem wit a thud.

He wuz dressd all n lether, frum his hed 2 his fut,
An he wuz cuvrd all ovr n ashs an sut.
A bundl o hash pieps he had strappd 2 his bak,
He lookd lack mi nabor jes cralld frum da sak.

His i's dey wur glazd an dey wur bludshot 2,
His faec wuz all rnkld an cuvrd wit goo.
His chappd lips dey wuz all rnkld an britl,
An his dirtee ol beerd wuz all mattd wit spitl.

A stump o a joint he had tiet n his teeth,
Da smoke it incircld his hed lack a reeth.
An ovr riep belee an his rinkld gont faec,
Tole mi all bout his losn da raec.

He wuz skinee an gont, a shore sien o mbibn,
I chortld an fartd n spite o miselfn.
His unstedee gaet an his twichn hed,
Suun tole he wuz drunk an stond ded.

He fartd and coffd, an startd his wurk,
Filld all da stokkins an ternd wit a jerk.
An layn his feengr aside o his faec,
An giveen a jerk, up da chimlee he raecd.

He slid 2 his slay 2 is teem gave a hollr,
Awaee dey all flue lack a drunkn ol yellr.
I herd him slur sloulee as he stumbld an fell,
Hapee Crismus 2 all an 2 all go ta hell!

With Love to My Wife

The night was very quiet and very still,
Tonight alone was I.
As I stood the lookout watch,
You could hear the seagulls cry.

The ship was moving slowly,
As slowly as it could.
Through the slowly rolling waves,
As I knew it would.

There is nothing in the sky or sea,
To catch my roving sight.
The shore was far off to my right,
And from it came a light.

I reported it and kept the watch,
I stood by and waited.
I thought of my lonely girl back home,
The one I'd always dated.

What's she doing now, I thought,
While I am out to sea?
My girl back home, she loves me so,
She is my wife-to-be.

A ring I had given her,
And my love for her proclaimed,
I hope to God, he keeps her safe,
And not to have her maimed.

The ship is due to pull in port,
The following afternoon,
I'll hit the beach and call her,
And whisper love's sweet croon.

The ship, it never made it,
It's simple mathematics,
Her memory is somewhere buried,
In a closet in an attic.

All hands went down –
No one was saved –
My girl was badly shaken;
And I know that she had prayed.

For I was washed ashore,
Alive but unconscious.
Now, our lives mean more to us,
Nothing can come between us.

We're married and I am still,
In care of Uncle Sam.
And now that my life is full of joy,
I could really give a damn.

The door of life was opened once,
And proudly I walked through,
There's nothing you can say to me –
There's nothing I won't do.

To make my wife so proud of me,
And see her look of joy.
Because she means my life to me,
Not just a simple toy.

To Be In Love This Way

How wonderful it must be,
To be in love this way.
When the love we both share,
Grows stronger with each passing day.

Someday I'm sure we'll be,
United by an unbreakable tie.
To share together the joys and strife of marriage life.

The ancient words "I love you" mean,
Nothing unless you mean them;
I think you do – I think I do,
Time will reveal the truth.

Whenever I'm sad or feeling blue,
Your love and joy will see me through.
Happiness will be ours and we will profit greatly.

The bonds of love will grow as the years go by,
And hold us together forever after.
And when you're in doubt, or not just right,
I'll be there to comfort you and make you happy.

For it is only right that our love should not die,
But flourish like a rosebud in the springtime.

Song Lyrics

And You keep right on Amazin'

I cry myself to sleep each night,
Wishing I could stop the plight.
I feel so helpless,
Without You by my side.

The Bible where your words are read,
Shows how to save my soul from dread.
And You keep right on amazin',
Since you've gone.

And You keep right on amazin',
Every minute of the day.
Every hour brings me closer,
To your kingdom.

And I can't help it, but I know,
I must go on.
And You keep right on amazin',
Since you've gone.

They say a man should never cry,
But on the cross I see you die.
My heart breaks down,
And sheds a million tears.

You died for me to set me free,
And faith is not a memory,
And You keep right on amazin'
Since you've gone.

And You keep right on amazin',
Every minute of the day.
Every hour brings me closer,
To your kingdom.

And I can't help it, but I know,
I must go on.
And You keep right on amazin',
Since you've gone.

God's Word is True

A long long time ago,
On a hill called Calvary.
A man was crucified,
For you and me.

God's word is true my friend,
It always has been.
Study and you will learn,
To overcome your sin.

He walked on Galilee,
The Prophets saw Him there.
He calmed down all their fears,
He showed His care.

God's word is true my friend,
It always has been.
Study and you will learn,
To overcome your sin.

He healed the sick and lame,
Prophets did too.
The demons fear His name,
He came for you.

God's word is true my friend,
It always has been.
Study and you will learn
To overcome your sin.

Despite our wickedness,
For us He cried.
His love for us is real –
For us He died.

God's word is true my friend,
It always has been.
Study and you will learn,
To overcome your sin.

He is longsuffering,
He wants to save us all.
Listen and hear my friend,
And heed the call.

God's word is true my friend,
It always has been.
Study and you will learn,
His love for you you'll see.

Cool-Aid

I went to a church service Sunday,
The preacher was ole' preacher Dan.
I heard the choir - they were singing,
A song about a very evil man.
I was offered a glass of their cool-aid,
And was offered to join with their clan.
With drink and food they were sharing,
With me, a poor preacher man.
Don't pour me a glass of your cool-aid,
For it is the worst in the land.
I'll keep on preaching the Gospel,
For I'm a poor preacher man.
I climbed into my old jalopy,
I Left there with tears in my eyes.
They were singing glories to satan,
And they were all teaching lies.
So, don't pour me a glass of your cool-aid,
For it is the worst in the land.
I'll keep on preaching the Gospel,
For I'm a poor preacher man.
No, don't pour me a glass of your cool-aid,
For it is the worst in the land.
I'll keep on preaching the Gospel,
For I'm a poor preacher man.

Yeah, I'm a poor preacher man.

Keep Your Eyes on Jesus

They saw Him on the water,
In the storm so very strong.
Their fear near overtook them,
They thought they had not long.

He said fear not for it is I—
Walking forward to them.
Peter said if so and He said come,
And he started to Him.

Keep your eyes on Jesus,
Keep your eyes on Him.
Keep your eyes on Jesus,
Only He can save your soul.

Peter's eyes were on Him,
The wind and waves were high.
As he left the boat and looked around,
He started sinking nigh.

Jesus reached and caught him,
Said little faith have ye.
He said why do you doubt me,
As He pulled him from the sea.

Keep your eyes on Jesus,
Keep your eyes on Him.
Keep your eyes on Jesus,
Only He can save your soul.

God Said to Them

God said to them
In the Garden of Eden,
All but one of this fruit shall you eat.

But the serpent came
And told them different,
They ate and they thought they were neat.

And then God said
depart from this Garden,
To wander all over this land.

N'er again to taste
The joys of heaven,
For your food you will work by your hand.

Then a Prophet's voice—
came from the far-land -
This is what it said:

The Son of God,
The Savior of the nations,
Lies in Jerusalem dead.

'Cause He came to save
A down fallen nation,
His word spread far and wide.

All have heard—
But few have listened,
To follow the path of His pride.

Jesus rose from the dead
To save us,
Unworthy as we may be.

Just trust and believe—
That is the gateway -
Eternity with Him you'll see.

Now all you Christians come and take a lesson,
From now on begin,
Always turn to Him,

And ask His forgiveness,
He will save you
And cleanse you from sin.

Narrow Roads

Almost Heaven Is for Christians,
If we follow the Lord Jesus.
Life is Harsh here because of satan,
All his wicked demons nipping at our heels.

Narrow Roads we go down,
To the place He is found.
Almost Heaven is for Christians,
With Him I'll be when I'm gone.

All my trials make me stronger,
All my worries He takes them all away.
Dark and lonely is satan's pathway,
Jesus turns the darkness into light.

Narrow Roads we go down,
To the place He is found.
Almost Heaven is for Christians,
With Him I'll be when I'm gone.

I hear His voice,
In the morning hours He tells me.
Reminds me that I have
A lovely home with Him.

And walking down the path,
I get a feeling that I
Should have done this
years ago... years ago...

Narrow Roads we go down,
To the place He is found.
Almost Heaven is for Christians.
With Him I'll be when I'm gone.

Narrow Roads we go down,
To the place He is found.
Almost Heaven is for Christians,
With Him I'll be when I'm gone.

With Him I'll be yes when I'm gone.

With Him I'll be yes when I'm gone.

Do You Know, You Are My Lifeline

He was standing in the courtyard,
Teaching the Gospel,
Knowing each and every heart.

He looked up and mentioned,
I stood there and listened,
To the words He did impart.

Do you know I am your lifeline?
He asked so quietly and low.
Do you know I am your lifeline?
Do you know what His voice did to me?

Ocean to ocean,
And border to border,
I looked for Him everywhere.

Searching the Scriptures,
Daily for the answers;
His Spirit leading me to truth.

He was gone just as quick,
As the wind on the meadow –
Leaving His Spirit with me.

Some day when I finally
Look up and see Him,
I know just what I'm going to say.

Do you know you are my lifeline?
Do you know what your dying did for me?
Do you know you are my lifeline?
And I praise Him each and every day.

Do you know you are my lifeline?
Do you know what your dying did for me?
Do you know you are my lifeline?
And I praise Him each and every day.

Do you know you are my lifeline?

I Want Your Love

Every night I hope and pray,
The Lord will teach me His way.
In His arms so big and strong,
I want to be forever long.

Because I want -
Your love - To call my own,
Yes I Want your love,
So I'll feel wanted all the time.

Precious Jesus, where are you?
With Your love oh so true.
And the love I can see
And have You near as you can be.

Because I want -
Your love - To call my own,
Yes I Want your love,
So I'll feel wanted all the time.

Some way and I know how,
I know You'll hear my plea.
Some way and I know how,
I'll have your love in me.

Dear Jesus, when you do,
I'll work and spread your love around.
That is all that I can do,
Till You come to take me home.

Because I want -
Your love - To call my own,
Yes I Want your love,
So I'll feel wanted all the time.

Dear Jesus, when you do,
I'll work and spread your love around.
That is all that I can do
Till You come to take me home.

Because I want -
Your love - To call my own,
Yes I want your love,
So I'll feel wanted all the time.

Please don't leave me,
I don't want to be alone.

Jesus, Yes My Savior

Born in a manger in Bethlehem,
To a humble servant of the Lord.
Raised in the word so He knew every line,
He preached in the temples in Jerusalem.

Jesus, Yes my Saviour,
King of all the world.

Through the known world He's walking along,
Teaching His Disciples the all in all,
The Pharisees said; who is this man?
He heals the sick and raises the dead?

Jesus, Yes my Saviour,
He paid for all my sins.

The Word was spread both far and wide
To the Jews and Gentiles alike
The Pharisees complain He violates the law
To hell with them, is what He saw.

Jesus, Yes my Saviour,
The only sinless man.

The Sabbath He worked the Pharisees led,
And He rebuked as the Prophets said.
They plotted in secret His life to take,
He foiled their plot His mission was laid.

Jesus, Yes my Saviour,
The man who knew no sin.

Casting out demons and spreading the Word,
The most amazing news the world ever heard.
Helping his servants and saving souls,
Healing men's bodies and making them whole.

Jesus, Yes my Saviour,
He paid for all my sin.

(Spoken)
His Kingdom is the biggest,
His Kingdom's the best.
The news He spread,
From the east to the west.
His disciples all went and spread it too,
Casting out demons with the power – They do.

They believed and followed even to death.
Sometimes weak and sometimes strong,
They even asked when will it be;
He said take your cross and follow me.

Jesus, Yes my Saviour,
King of all the world.

Near the end He was having a feast,
With his followers and serving their needs,
He said, remember me when I'm not here,
I'll send to you a Spirit for evermore.

Jesus, Yes my Saviour,
He paid for all my sins.

After the feast they captured Him.
Peter rebelled and He said no.
The word is true the time is come,
I have to go for it is so.

Jesus, Yes my Saviour,
He overcame the world.

He said that He'll return for us,
By faith we believe that this is so.
By believing and keeping His word we're saved,
And we'll be with Him eternally.

Jesus, Yes my Saviour,
The man who knew no sin.

Jesus, Yes my Saviour,
He overcame the world.

I'm Coming Back To Jesus Now

Well I went to a church meeting
Down the street,
The people down there they like to say
Just go away.

I'm on my way;
I'm coming back to Jesus now.

Talking with the devil
And have a good time.
Eating up his lies
And drinking his wine.

I'm on my way;
I'm coming back to Jesus now.

Now some folks say
The devil is good,
I caught him truthing
As if he could,

I'm on my way;
I'm coming back to Jesus now.

Here come his minions
Down the street,
With lying eyes
My soul to steal.

I'm on my way;
I'm coming back to Jesus now.

Here comes the devil
Walking down the street,
With slicked up shoes
Resting on his feet.

(spoken)
Good morning satan, stand over there
Shuffle quick now!
Hello satan I know you
In your snappy suit and your shiny shoes.

I'm on my way;
I'm coming back to Jesus now.

When I get ready
To leave this earth,
I'll look back and see
The devil's worth.

I'm on my way;
I'm coming back to Jesus now.

Yeah I'm coming back to Jesus now.

Blessings by the Number

Blessing number one,
Was when He died for me.
I did not know,
I could be loved this way.

Blessing number two,
Was when He rose from the dead,
He rose so I
Could live eternally.

Now, I've got blessings by the number,
A love that I can't lose.
Every day I praise His name –
Each day I love Him more.

Yes, I've got blessings by the number,
A love that I can't lose,
And the day that I stop counting,
With Jesus I will be.

Blessing number three,
Was when He told me,
He promised me a teacher
That would stay.

With swelling heart,
I gladly do His bidding,
I'm very glad to join
Him every day.

53

Now, I've got blessings by the number,
A love that I can't lose.
Every day I praise His name –
Each day I love Him more.

Yes, I've got blessings by the number,
A love that I can't lose,
And the day that I stop counting,
With Jesus I will be.

Yeah, the day that I stop counting,
With Jesus I will be.

I'm Glad I Have My God

At my door the Lord is knocking,
His warm breath I can feel.
His Son is close beside me,
I'm glad I have my God.

I go out for to witness,
Find satan hard at work,
And I find a poor lost soul mate,
That Jesus lead me to.

I see the devil's destruction,
I see it everywhere,
I try to keep from sinning,
I have His forgiveness there.

I'm glad I work for Jesus,
And enjoy the work I do,
His Spirit is close inside me,
I'm glad I have my God.

I see the devil's destruction,
I see it everywhere,
I try to keep from sinning,
I have His forgiveness there.

I'm glad I work for Jesus,
And enjoy the work I do,
His Spirit is close inside me,
I'm glad I have my God.

Eyeball Shootout

From the great Atlantic Ocean,
To the wide Pacific shore,
Big rigs were a rollin',
Sucking diesel – more.

From rice rockets sipping ethanol,
And mid-size suburban vans,
Neither rain nor wind nor dark of night,
Will deter them from their plans.

Listen to the static,
The crackle and the squall.
As they fly along the highways,
Through the plains and trees so tall.

Hear the might roar of diesels,
The vans they whisper all.
We're traveling thru the jungles,
To the Century Club Eyeball.

Big rigs and rice rockets,
And even vans I hear,
They were all a'headin'
To the city of De Pere.

They slowly congregated,
Tall tales were freely told.
Of escapades of glory,
From participants of old.

Listen to the static,
The crackle and the squall.
As they fly along the highways,
Through the plains and trees so tall.

Hear the might roar of diesels,
The vans they whisper all.
We're traveling thru the jungles
To the Century Club Eyeball.

The air was charged with static,
The anticipation grew.
To see which one would be the best,
They all thought they knew.

The crowd they all grew quiet,
As the first one came on-line.
Tweaking, squeaking, testing,
They knew it was the time.

Listen to the static,
the crackle and the squall,
As they fly along the highways,
Through the plains and trees so tall.

Hear the might roar of diesels,
The vans they whisper all.
We're traveling thru the jungles,
To the Century Club Eyeball.

They pulled into the open field,
Ready for the test.
The radios locked, antennas loaded –
Hoping for the best.

The first one keys up a carrier –
The shootout has begun
The last one unkeys the carrier,
The shootout has been won!

Listen to the static,
The crackle and the squall.
As they fly along the highways,
Through the plains and trees so tall.

Hear the might roar of diesels,
The vans they whisper all.
We're traveling thru the jungles
To the Century Club Eyeball.

He joins the ranks of winners past
His efforts not in vain
May his fame and glory –
Live on and never wane.

May he always have a signal strong
And be heard by one and all
And for the station calling him
Through static hear his call.

Listen to the static,
The crackle and the squall.
As they fly along the highways,
Through the plains and trees so tall.

Hear the might roar of diesels,
The vans they whisper all.
We're traveling thru the jungles,
To the Century Club Eyeball.

Light Upon My Path

One day he was passing,
I caught him comin' by.
To look this poor man over,
Under God's blue sky.

I only stood there weeping,
As I was lookin' back,
He just left me crying,
By Your light upon my path.

Hello, Jesus. Until I come back home,
You'll be my dream.
Hello, Jesus. All my sins,
You have forgiven me.

I'm gonna follow Jesus,
I ask Him what I lack.
We'll leave satan running,
From Your light upon my path.

I always look to Jesus,
It helps me when I'm blue.
I know that I love Him,
That's all I want to do.

Satan cannot settle down,
Because he has to roam.
And when I hear him coming close,
I've gotta move along.

Hello, Jesus. There's something down the
Path keeps calling me,
Hello, Jesus. I guess that's just
the Spirit's way to be,

So when I get that feeling,
He won't hold me back.
We're gonna leave him running,
From Your light upon my path.

I know Jesus loves me,
I love Jesus too.
And He understands me,
When I'm feeling blue.

When I hear him coming close,
I take up all the slack.
We're gonna leave him running,
From Your light upon my path.

Hello, Jesus. You'll not leave me,
But I gotta know.
Hello, Jesus, he's coming,
I can hear his minions low.

They'll be here in a minute,
we'll wave and not look back.
We're gonna leave them running,
From Your light upon my path.

I hear Jesus calling

I hear Jesus calling,
homesick tears are falling,
I've been away from Jesus far too long.

I'm gonna have a cheerful mind,
When I cross that Jesus line,
I hear Jesus calling me back home.

I recall that very day,
they said son don't go that way,
Now I'm glad I didn't listen to their call.

I don't miss my mom and dad,
or the good friends that I had,
Cause I have the Holy Spirit for my all.

I hear Jesus calling,
homesick tears are falling,
I've been away from Jesus far too long.

I'm gonna have a cheerful mind,
When I cross that Jesus line,
I hear Jesus calling me back home.

I've been through a thousand trials,
mostly beat up all around.
And the glorious victory of Jesus has not gone.

I've been hungry and I've been cold,
And was troubled in my soul.
Now I'm on that Jesus train a' headed home.

I hear Jesus calling,
homesick tears are falling,
I've been away from Jesus far too long.

I'm gonna have a cheerful mind,
When I cross that Jesus line,
I hear Jesus calling me back home.

I'm Not Satan

I'm not satan, My name is Jesus.
Satan's with us still today.
His eyes are not blue,
His eyes are fiery red.
He will be with us until the end.

He was once the Morning light,
His lies went through the night.
Your lust for earthly things,
Grew with each passing day.

Then one sunny day,
He led you all astray.
He left your soul drowning in your sin.
And you've been for years.

Crying satan, satan.

I'm not satan, My name is Jesus.
Satan's with us still today.
His eyes are not blue,
His eyes are fiery red.
He will be with us until the end.

I'm Not satan

In The Strong Arms of Jesus

Spend all your time working,
for the Lord Jesus Christ,
For a place that will make it okay.
There's always a reason

To follow satan's deceit,
And it's hard, at the end of the day.
I need His warm comfort, oh beauty divine.
Love words cry from my heart.
Let me be empty, oh and weightless, I will.
I'll find my peace with Him.

(Chorus)
In the strong arms of Jesus,
Fly away from here,
From this dark sinful world,
And the destruction that is near.
You are not of this world,
My Father gave you to me.
In the strong arms of Jesus,
You'll find comfort you see.

So tired of the troubles,
Everywhere you turn,
There's satan and his liars at your back.
Satan keeps on twisting,
Keeps on building the lies.
The Spirit makes up for all that you lack.

It makes a difference,
Jesus is your only chance,
It's easy to believe -
In satan's madness,
Oh, his glorious radiance
Brings tears to my eyes.

(Chorus)
In the strong arms of Jesus,
Fly away from here,
From this dark sinful world,
And the destruction that is near.
You are not of this world,
My Father gave you to me.
In the strong arms of Jesus,
You'll find comfort you see.

In the strong arms of Jesus,
You'll find comfort you see.

The Spirit Keeps on Teaching

I Close My Eyes to picture,
What Heaven must likely be.
From golden streets to walk upon,
And emeralds to see.

I see the living rivers,
And the angels from above.
I see Jesus walking there,
Showering all with love.

But most of all I see the love,
That everybody shares.
And best of all He sent His Son,
To take away my cares.

I wish that I could spend an hour,
At Jesus precious feet,
The Spirit keeps on teaching
The mind of God to me.

How I wish to hear the words,
For everyone to share,
The Prophets and the angels,
Share the scenery so fair,

To be a part of all this love,
For all eternity.
I would walk through hell to have,
His love for all to see.

But most of all I see the love,
That everybody shares.
And best of all He sent His Son,
To take away my cares.

I wish that I could spend an hour,
At Jesus precious feet,
The Spirit keeps on teaching,
The mind of God to me.

My God

(My God, Our God)
Every morning in our prayer room, We ask for His grace,
Praying and asking For His forgiveness so great.
We thank Him for sending His Son from above,
And beg Him to shower us With
mercy and love. (from God)

(My God, Our God) Our great God (Our God)

No one seemed to care Where Jesus came from,
He was born of a virgin So humble and low.
The angels proclaimed – The shepherds said nigh,
They were tending their flocks, In
the green fields nearby.
(My God)

The Magi asked – About the word of the news,
The one who was born – The King of the Jews?
In Bethlehem, Was the word they were given,
To Him went the Magi, Their gifts
they delivered. (Our God)

(My God, Our God) Our great God (Our God)

In the temple they sold, To the crowd in the town,
They peddled their wares, But not for a crown.
The crashing sound, Of the tables turned over,
Left little doubt They worshipped their lovers – Not God

The merchants and priests, Through
the dust and the dung,
Just stood there agape, In shame their heads hung.
He stood among men – The strength of a tower,
He came from Heaven, His love
for to shower – (My God)

(My God, Our God) Our great God (Our God)

Then came the rumble Somewhere in the crowd,
They cried crucify him, We don't want him around!
The guards they took Him And locked Him away,
No one would save Him, No one would say – My God.

Every year we remember - Every year we proclaim,
On this cross died a just man For our sins He was slain.
The Christians are saying Follow Jesus today,
For He is the light And He is the way. (My God)

(My God, Our God) Our great God (Our God)

Martial Law Is Coming To Town

You'd better watch out You'd better not fly,
Have your guns loaded I'm telling you why,
Martial law is comin' to town.

They're making a list And checking who's got,
Gonna find out who's ready or not,
martial law is comin' to town.

They see you when you're sleepin',
They see when you're awake.
They know what you've been talking about,
So be careful what you say.

You'd better watch out You'd better not fly,
Have your guns loaded I'm telling you why,
Martial law is comin' to town.

They're opening camps And fillin' em full,
Gonna make sure, you're beheaded or dull,
Martial law is comin' to town.

They'll get you when you're sleeping,
Even when you're awake.
They know where you'll be hiding out,
So keep watch for your sake.

You'd better watch out You'd better not fly,
Have your guns loaded I'm telling you why,
Martial law is comin' to town.

They're movin' a train And loadin' 'em up,
Homeless - terrorists ready or not,
Martial law is comin' to town.

Martial law is comin' -
Martial law is comin' -
Martial law is comin' to town.

Short Stories

The Building

It had been vacant for years. The metal "For Sale" sign in front had turned red from oxidation. From the flapping shutters framing broken glass to the peeling paint and the cracked sidewalk, the signs of neglect screamed out. The flower gardens were overgrown with weeds and struggling to survive. The lawn had long since given up the fight to survive and the grass had receded into scattered small patches. The swings swayed from unseen children playing. The weeds had successfully claimed the area under and around them. I continued walking the property and more signs of neglect surfaced. The fence bore scars from the years of neglect and vandalism. The cracks in the drive had filled with small saplings, splitting it further. Clumps of dandelions and grass dotted the surface where it split from neglect and weather.

I walked up the rickety steps to the dilapidated front door, standing slightly ajar. I pushed it open to the sound of squeaky rusting hinges. Once inside, a deafening silence assaulted my ears. The dimly lit interior belied the fact of the bright sunlight outside. As my eyes adjusted to the dimness, I saw the leaves and dirt that littered the floor, blown in through the broken windows. My inspection continued past a group of metal chairs and around the main room. More signs of neglect and vandalism. The furniture arranged haphazardly in small groups, presumably for small intimate conversations. I progressed through an open door at the other side. More neglect. This area had seen its better days. Dirt and leaves dusted the floor in the same fashion as the previous room. I continued my inspection through the rest of the rooms and saw the same desolation, neglect and vandalism. The alphabet soup of organizations had failed this once beautiful building. Vandalism and weather had taken its toll. Cracked porcelain, dry rotted furniture and uneven floors were abundant evidence.

A monumental task to refurbish it I thought as I continued my inspection. I wandered around through the rest o the rooms, and finally found myself back at the entryway. I walked through the door, squinting from the onslaught of the bright sunlight. I walked out far enough to view the roof. Missing shingles left splotches of the sub roof exposed and confirmed the water damage seen inside. A wrought iron bench with the paint peeling and exposing the metal underneath sat forlornly off to one side. I walked over and sat down, thinking. The building had only been vacant for five years and it needs extensive repairs I said aloud to no one in particular. Finally, after a long thoughtful contemplation, I screwed up my courage and said, "I'll take it."

The church will once again see the love it had known in days gone by.

The Elephant Tree

She stood in the window, looking out at the bleak landscape. She could feel the cold on the panes, and was glad she was inside the house. The yard was barren but for a lone tree off to the right. The tree looked like a grotesque animal with shiny white fur. She dubbed it the elephant tree. When they were in India, she had her own elephant to ride. It had been a small one, but to her it was a huge animal. She had become attached to it, and was sad to leave it when they left. She had named it Ben. The tree reminded her of Ben, only this had shimmering white skin. "Ben," she whispered, "You are still here for me to talk to."

It was getting late, she thought, and her father would be home soon. Her mother had died when she was two. Her father never married again. She turned from the window and looked around the large room. The room was decorated with wooden oak paneling with a fireplace in the center of the far wall. A crackling fire was burning, keeping the cold that seeped through the window at bay and throwing weaving shadows on the wall. The tall drapes covering the windows also helped to keep the cold outside from entering the room. A sofa was nestled along the left wall and a long coffee table was placed in front of it. The striped pattern reminded her of a white tiger. A tall suit of armor stood on the right side of the sofa. It was only six feet tall, but it towered over her by three feet. Opposite the table were two matching chairs. Along another wall was a set of floor to ceiling bookcases loaded with books. She climbed part way up the ladder that stretched to the ceiling, riding on thin rails at the top and wheels at the bottom. Pushing herself along, the book spines caught the rays of the fire and sparkled like gold and silver. It reminded her of the library at her school, although the books in the school library didn't sparkle like that. She was fascinated by books. In the far corner she could see a large globe set in a base. She walked over to it and discovered the globe turned on some invisible pivot in two directions at once. The globe was almost two feet in diameter with a base of wood. She stared at the globe and its coloring. The continents were green and brown, and the oceans were blue. The words were unfamiliar to her. They didn't match any of the words and numbers she had learned in school. She was in the fourth grade and enjoyed learning about writing, history, science, and math. She was in the library of the big house. The wood double doors in the library led to the main portion of the house, which was on the first floor.

She left the study and saw the double staircase leading to the second floor. That is where the bedrooms were. She went through the door to the right, into the dining room. A large rectangular table of wood that shined and glittered under the chandelier over the table greeted her. The chandelier had candles in it. The table was lined on both sides with chairs. At the head of the table was a chair she had seen pictures of in her history books. It was a chair that she remembered seeing in a picture with a king in it. An English king, if she remembered correctly. There was a fireplace in here too. Her father had told her the house had fireplaces in all the rooms for heat. Her bedroom upstairs had its own fireplace. The silverware and dishes adorning the table reflected the light and sparkled like jewels.

Her father was an archeologist. They had arrived three days before amidst a snowstorm. She had not had time to do any exploring.

The first two days were spent unpacking. Today she had nothing to do but wander around the house. She yearned to go outside to play, but her father cautioned her not to go out alone as the weather here could get bad quickly. They were at a house that belonged to a friend of her father's, also an archeologist. He was somewhere in the Yucatan, her father said, and they would have the house to themselves except for the help. She didn't know where that was, but surmised it was far away.

She went into the kitchen, where the cook was putting the finishing touches on dinner. She was a short woman with white hair gathered in a bun on the back of her head. She had a white apron that covered a floral dress. She had learned her name was Helga and she told her she had been the cook there for years. In the middle of the room was a huge square table covered with steaming dishes filled with food, ready to be whisked into the dining room. The dishes matched the dinnerware already on the table in the dining room. Helga was removing bread from the oven when she arrived.

"Dinner will be ready soon, honey. Go tell your father, he just arrived," said Helga in a thick accent she couldn't identify.

"Okay." She left the kitchen and went upstairs to her father's room and knocked on the door. It was opened immediately and she was greeted warmly by her father. Her father was a big man, standing over six feet tall. He had broad shoulders and a thin waist. His arms were the size of a bear's.

"What has my Punkin doing all day while I was away?" he asked as he picked her up and gave her a big hug. "I missed you today."

"I was exploring the house. It is a very big house," she replied. "Helga said that dinner is almost ready," she continued.

"Well, let's not keep her waiting, shall we?" he countered, and started for the door.

At that, they headed for the dining room. When they arrive in the dining room, Helga had already begun placing the steaming dishes on the table. There were green and yellow vegetables, which she only recognized the corn. Roast duck was the main course. Helga served the duck and placed the vegetables on their plates.

"You have a birthday coming up, don't you?" Her father asked.

"Yes, I'll be ten years old in four days," she replied.

"Tomorrow we will go into town and get you into the local school. We'll be here for a while," her father said.

"I can hardly wait. I love school," she said. She loved to learn new things and read about faraway places, some of which she had already seen at her tender age.

"I have a birthday present for you in my pocket," he said. He reached in his pocket and removed a box from it and handed it to her.

She opened the box and exclaimed, "I love it! Thanks!" Her father had given her a watch. It had Roman numerals for the ordinate numbers, and dots for the rest. It had black hour and minute hands shaped like arrows. The gold case and matching gold band shimmered from the candles. It was beautiful.

The next day dawned bright with the sun bouncing off the snow and making everything sparkle like a many-faceted jewel. Her father took her to school and after she was registered, he left to go the university where he worked. After school, she walked home, as it wasn't far. She enjoyed the crunch of the snow under her boots. The sky was clear; there was no sign of a storm. She was half way home when a storm hit with sudden ferocity. Visibility dropped to almost nothing. She continued on her way, thinking she knew the way.

She wandered around and soon found herself hopelessly lost. She stopped and tried to find her way, but it was no use, she could see nothing past the whirling snow. She diverted her way to where she thought was a house. It turned out to be a mistake, as she slipped and fell into a culvert. The culvert was deep, almost ten feet deep, and the sides were almost vertical. She had scraped her legs on the side as she descended. She landed on the bottom with a crash. She had banged her head on the descent and blacked out. When she regained consciousness, she looked around her. Then she felt the pain in her leg. It was twisted in an unnatural angle, and hurt badly. She tried to stand up, but the pain made her fall down. She feared it might be broken. She called out but no one was around to hear her. She soon realized she was stuck and no one knew where she was, and she became afraid.

She didn't know where she was. She began to cry. She didn't know how long she had been there, but the cold was seeping into her coat and she was getting cold. She thought of her father and Helga. They would come looking for her when she didn't arrive from school when they expected her. She couldn't move very well, as her leg was hurting badly by now. She thought of the elephant tree, and was able to get herself calmed down somewhat. She was still scared. What if no one found her? She drifted in and out of consciousness. She was getting colder. Her fingers were cold and she had lost feeling in them. She could no longer feel her feet. She didn't know how long she had been there, it seemed like an eternity. She had her watch her father had bought for her. It had been almost three hours since she had fallen into the culvert. The storm was blowing the snow around so she could only see her feet. The wind had picked up and was blowing more fiercely. She had dressed warm that morning; she had leggings, a heavy coat and mittens. Her head was covered with a woolen cap and she pulled it down over her ears to keep them warm. She began shivering from the cold.

The elephant with silver skin will find her she thought. She was getting colder. She drifted into unconsciousness again. When she regained conscious, the wind had died down, and was almost quiet. She called out loudly to no one in particular. Although she thought she was yelling loudly, it came out as only a whisper. Her lips were frozen. She was becoming hysterical. She struggled to look at her watch, and saw it had been over five hours since she had fallen into the culvert. She could not feel her legs. She was shivering constantly now. She drifted into unconsciousness again. She began dreaming about the elephant tree. The elephant was looking for her, she hoped. She called out, but the elephant tree didn't hear her through the howling wind.

She groaned. She was in pain all over. She was no longer cold, but felt warm all over. She saw the elephant tree and it seemed to be smiling at her. Then it suddenly trumpeted and disappeared, only to be replaced by her father.

She slowly opened her eyes and found herself in a bed. She was covered in blankets and a nurse was standing over her.

"She opened her eyes. She's awake," the nurse said.

Her father, who had been sitting in the chair across the room jumped up and rushed to the bed, his face contorted in concern. She found she could not move her leg. The sun was streaming through the window and she discovered it was daylight.

John V. Spillman

"Will she be okay?" Her father asked the nurse.

"She will be fine, Sir. She was in the cold weather for over six hours, but she will recover," the nurse replied.

Her father's face changed from concern to relief.

The Last Ride

I looked up as the door squeaked open to reveal a petite woman with shoulder length auburn hair, sparkling azure eyes and a laughing smile. Heat and dust preceded her through the door. We had been seeing each other for several months. I finally screwed up my courage and asked her to marry me two weeks earlier and she had said yes, and a week later, moved from the hotel to her house at the edge of town.

"Hello Louise. What brings you out in this God awful heat this late in the afternoon?" I got up from my chair and met her halfway across the room for an embrace and a lingering kiss. She looked lovely in her flowing burgundy dress and white bodice.

"Just came by to see my love and see if he was going to take me to the dance this evening," she replied.

"If that's an invite, I cannot refuse," I laughed. "I'll be finished soon if you care to wait."

"I'd be happy to. I received a letter from Sammy today; she is coming in on the stage on the twenty-ninth. She was ecstatic when I asked her to be my maid of honor," she said moving the chair closer to my desk.

"I wrote to my family, and my daughter and her family will be here by the end of the month. My two sons and daughter will also be here," I said.

"Is Sammy's husband and children coming with her?"

"Yes, As a matter of fact, they are." She wanted her daughter to be her maid of honor and I agreed. She had spent a month with Samantha when her daughter was born. She had named her Alice after her maternal grandmother. She lives in Texas with her husband Sam Trent. They have two children, a son and daughter. They had been married for twelve years and the children were ten and eleven now.

"Then we can schedule the wedding for the first?" I asked.

"That would be perfect."

"Okay, let's go. I'm finished."

After straightening my desk, we headed for the door. I locked the door and we walked slowly hand in hand toward our home, making small talk.

The first thing I did when we arrived home was fill the tub with hot water for a bath. Louise was thoughtful enough to have water heated for just that purpose. After soaking for a long while, letting my muscles relax, and after the water had cooled off, I got out and dried off with a large fluffy towel. I dressed in my finest clothes and went to the kitchen where Louise had finished preparing the evening meal. Everything smelled good. I sat down to a dinner of roast chicken, rolls and corn. For dessert, she had baked a cherry pie – my favorite.

"You're going to spoil me yet," I said.

"That's the idea," she replied, laughing.

I cleaned the dishes and put them away while Louise readied herself for the dance. We arrived at the Town Hall shortly before the dance started, and found Roy standing in a group of men near the door.

I went over to the group, and after greetings were exchanged all around, I said, "Roy, I'd like to talk to you for a minute, if you could spare the time."

"Okay," he said, and left the group and walked over to where Louise was talking with a group of the women.

"Hello ladies," I said. "Could I pry my lady from your grasp for a short while," I asked.

"Certainly Sheriff," they chorused in unison.

I related to him that Louise had agreed to marry me, and would he officiate it on the first of the month. He congratulated us and heartily agreed. They laughed and exchanged small talk for a time, and then merged into the gathering crowd. The musicians were tuning their instruments, indicating the dance was beginning.

After a couple of two-steps and several waltzes, Louise said, "The band is exceptionally good tonight."

"Yes, I have to agree with you on that," I replied.

They played several more two-steps and waltzes, and then played some square dance music for the older folks in the crowd to enjoy. The refreshments and sandwiches were quickly disappearing and everyone was thoroughly enjoying themselves.

Around midnight, the band played a last "ladies choice" waltz, began packing up their instruments and left soon after.

As we were walking slowly back to our house, Robert came running up to them. "Charlie, the bank has been robbed and Donald was killed," he blurted breathlessly.

"Do you know who did it?" I asked.

"A man named Roy Richy. The ace of spades was found on his chest," he wheezed.

"That's Roy's trademark all right. Do you know which way he went?"

"There was a hand-drawn arrow pointing to the left on the card," he said.

"That means he is headed west. That is part of his trademark too," I said and continued, "He's a slippery one – most of the sheriffs in Kansas were looking for him. I will start after him at first light. It's too late to do anything tonight."

I was up before the sun to get an early start. Louise was still asleep, and I silently strapped on my guns, filled my saddlebag with food and other essentials, and headed for the stable. The sun was just peeking over the horizon when I climbed onto my horse and started out. The blazing sun rapidly pushed away the cool of the night, even at this early hour. It was going to be a hot dusty day, I thought. The horse's hooves were stirring up clouds of dust as I headed west out of town. There was no breeze to disturb the trail and it was easy to follow in the daylight. By early afternoon, I stopped to take a break. I let my horse wander and nibble on the prairie sandreed while I took a long draw on my canteen. I wiped my sweaty brow with my bandana, took my tobacco pouch and papers from my shirt pocket, rolled a cigarette and lit it with one of the precious matches I had. Matches were a new invention and expensive. A slight breeze pushing the fluffy clouds westward did nothing to relieve the burning heat of the sun. I pushed on until I saw a group of desert willow in the distance. A good place to rest for the night, I thought.

I watched the ominous clouds billow higher and turn dark in the early evening sky. Soon they would be full-fledged storm clouds. We could use some rain, I thought, although it would make it harder to track my quarry. It had been more than a month since the last rain. The bleak desert with arroyos and light hills sparsely covered with sage bushes, prairie sandreed and creosote trees could use some moisture. There were lightning flashes within the louds as they came closer, pushed by the quickening wind. The breeze became brisker and the sandy soil became miniature tornado like spouts that danced across the landscape. I walked over to my horse, a chestnut, removed the saddle and blanket and placed them on the ground. I gathered firewood from the sparse pickings and using my flint and steel, nursed the fire to life. The small grove of desert willow would protect them from the worst of the storm, should it materialize. Although the storm clouds moved slowly, the air held no hint of rain.

The night came quickly and the quickening wind whipped the flickering flames of the fire – the only light left – while the storm clouds hid the moon and stars. I placed my 1869 Schofield pistol and my 1873 Winchester Henry repeating rifle under the bedroll to protect them from the worst of the storm, should it materialize. I prepared the jackrabbit I had killed earlier in the day for the fire. After eating and washing it down with a draw on my dented canteen, I pulled my tobacco pouch and cigarette papers from my shirt pocket and rolled a cigarette. I thought about my partner and best friend George. He was killed in a raid between some settlers and a band of renegade Comanche north of Abilene a month ago, and I still grieved. We had been friends from childhood. I did not have the spirit to replace him with another partner yet. Upon finishing my smoke, I removed my boots and crawled into my bedroll, covered my craggy face with my brown weather-beaten Stetson and soon fell into a troubled sleep.

The morning dawned bright and hot. No rain had come during the night and the air was dry and gritty. I fed my horse and finished the jackrabbit left over from the previous evening's meal. I saddled up and continued my westward trek. After several hours, I spotted a jackrabbit. I grabbed my rifle and taking careful aim, soon bagged it. I alit from my horse, gathered and dressed it. I then got back on my horse and continued on my way. The landscape was gradually changing as more sage bushes, prairie grass and larger groves of creosote trees appeared. The ground was getting less sandy, making it harder to track. I hoped I was getting closer to my quarry. I spotted a water hole surrounded by a grove of creosote trees and filled both canteens. I allowed my horse to drink its fill and nibble on the grass nearby. I wiped my sweaty brow with my already soaked bandana. Looking around, I spotted the remains of a cold campfire. I am still going in the right direction. I wondered what Louise was doing right now. It sure would be good to be back with her. I rested for a spell longer and set off again. The sun was high in the sky and burned ferociously. My bulky frame was soaked in sweat and uncomfortable, but I continued.

I had a one hundred percent success rate of capturing my quarry and was confident I would succeed again. I had been a Ranger for almost ten years, recruited from the Cavalry after attaining the rank of Colonel, and doubled for the sheriff of the town. I am almost fifty years old and considered retiring. We could live comfortably on my cavalry pension. With the resignation papers in my pocket, I intended to tender them when I returned. With the railroad finished at Promontory, Utah several years earlier, the west was changing. The railroad brought more settlers from the East and with the Indians confined to the reservations; the cavalry had little left to do. The treaty allowed the Comanche to hunt the buffalo, but mostly they staged raids on the settlers. Time weighed heavily and I began reminiscing about the past again. I had married my childhood sweetheart Mary Thorton while still a Lieutenant. She blessed me with two strapping sons and a lovely daughter. She died just before I made Captain. Our daughter Sylvia lives in Virginia with her husband, George Armstrong, a Lieutenant in the cavalry. They have two daughters, Felicity and Grace, two lovely granddaughters. My sons Charlie Jr. and Trent enlisted in the Cavalry and stationed two days ride away. They both attained the rank of Lieutenant quickly and enjoy the single life of a cavalry soldier.

The going was uneventful, only the rolling landscape provided some relief from the monotony. After another hour of riding, I came upon Roy's campsite he used the night before, the ashes cold. I could tell by the tracks that Roy's horse had lost a shoe and would be traveling slower now. The ground was getting rockier and the hills more frequent. I topped the latest hill to reveal an expanse of open range covered in buffalo grass and a few large creosote trees. I pulled my binoculars from their well-worn leather pouch and scanned the range. Off to the south was a small herd of buffalo. The Comanche would be hunting in that area. I took a long draw on my battered canteen and picked my way slowly down the rocky hill. The sun was almost directly overhead in the cloudless sky. A half hour later, I reached the grassy plain and started across.

I was making good time when a group of six Comanche warriors rode up on colorful mustangs with no saddles and surrounded me with nocked arrows. The leader was the only one with a rifle – a Winchester repeater decorated with feathers and leather fringe. A buffalo hunting party, I guessed. Colorful paint decorated most of their upper bodies and faces, and they wore breechcloths and fringed leggings. They all wore a feather in their hair, and the leader had several in his. The leader sat tall on his horse and appeared older than the rest. The rest looked to be no older than sixteen summers. I had dealt with the Comanche before, knew some of them spoke English so was not worried.

"Hagani'yunde eN gaH takwa? eyu?" the leader said.

I shrugged my shoulders and said, "No speak Comanche. Speak English."

They all looked at the leader. After a few minutes of pregnant silence, one of the braves spoke, "Me speak English. Me Running Wolf, leader Brave Eagle. Speak no English." He conferred with Brave Eagle for a long time and then he spoke again, "Brave Eagle want to know why you on Comanche land."

"Follow bad man," pointing to the west toward Roy. "Me Ranger. Name is Charlie," showing them my badge. "Catch bad man and take him back to stand trial for murder."

With the braves getting restless as indicated by their nervous movements, Running Wolf and Brave Eagle conferred in their native tongue briefly, although it seemed a long time.

Running Wolf then looked in my direction and said, "Go now. Brave Eagle say you can pass."

The braves lowered their bows and returned their arrows to their quiver. Without another word, they turned as one, sped off toward the south and was soon lost to sight.

I let my horse graze while I took a long draw on my canteen, smoked a cigarette and wiped my sweaty face before setting off again. Fluffy white clouds scampered across the sky from the east. The pockmarked ground had prairie dog holes, so I let my horse amble on its own, but controlled its direction. It was a good horse; the cavalry let me keep it when I left. It was very slow going, and I led the horse toward a tall creosote tree in the near distance. Three hours later, I stretched out under the tree and wiped my brow again. My mind drifted back again to the past. With George gone, I had only Louise and my children left.

With the sun getting lower in the sky, I decided to camp here for the night. I found enough firewood for a fire, and soon had one burning. I fixed a spit from the branches and cooked the rabbit I had shot earlier, and ate in brooding silence. The bright stars and full moon made eerie shadows across the plain. I watched them without seeing them for a long time. The breeze was getting cooler, a nice change from the oppressive heat. I tended my horse and prepared my bedroll, but sleep was a long time coming.

I woke the next morning before the sun came up. I fixed the fire, made a pot of coffee, smoked a cigarette and watched the sunrise. The sun, peeking over the hills bathed the scene in a gradually brightening orange. A kaleidoscope of oranges, yellows and reds soon streaked the sky. It was beautiful. I wished I were enjoying it with Louise. I cleaned up camp and set off toward the west. The sun brought the oppressive heat from the day before.

He traveled slower and by noon had reached the edge of the plain.

I followed Roy's tracks into a narrow pass with almost vertical sides. When I had almost reached the other end of the long pass, a shot rang out. Rock fragments showered me and I quickly dismounted. With little protective cover, I moved to the side away from the direction of the shot. I scanned the rocky face to locate the shooter- it had to be Roy. The glint from his rifle revealed him half way up the right side of the pass. With one eye on Roy's position, I retrieved my rifle from its scabbard and quickly retreated to safety. Another shot rang out and the bullet hit the wall above me. The next shot from Ray found its mark. The bullet went deep into my shoulder, spewing blood. In no time, my shirt was soaked with blood. I was getting dizzy and fell down. I could still see Roy in this position. After what seemed an eternity, Roy was standing over me.

He laughed a raspy laugh and said, "Good-bye Ranger."

He pointed his rifle at my head but I got off a shot first and my aim was true. He stood there with a surprised look on his face for a moment and then collapsed.

I lay there for a long time, drifting in and out of consciousness. It was dark when I finally became more aware of my situation. I crawled painfully over to my horse, raised myself up by the stirrup, and retrieved my saddlebags. I rummaged through them, got my medical kit and dressed I dressed my wound as best I could. It was not as bad as I had originally thought. The bullet had gone all the way through and did not hit bone. I lay here for a long time, eventually worked my way over to my horse and tried to mount it. I was overwhelmed by nausea and dizziness and passed out. When I came to again, it was getting light. After several failed attempts, I final succeeded in mounting the horse. I found Ray's horse with the bank money, grabbed the reins and headed back toward town. It was going to be a long ride home.

The cloudless sky gave no respite from the burning heat. I made good time and arrived at the campsite from the day before. My shoulder was hurting terribly. I removed the bandages and cleaned the wound as best I could which had become red and puffy. I took a cartridge from my belt, removed the lead, poured the powder into the wound and lit it with one of the few matches I had left. The pain was excruciating. I gritted my teeth, and after a long while, the pain subsided some. Slowly and painfully I redressed the wound as best I could and chewed on some jerky from my saddlebags. No hot meal tonight, I thought. He rolled a cigarette and smoked it. Using my saddlebags as a pillow, I drifted into and out of a feverish restless sleep.

My shoulder pain finally woke me from my dreamless sleep. I mounted my horse slowly and gathering the reins from Roy's horse, continued on my way, the sun shining brightly in the cloudless sky. I was still five days away from town and hoped I would make it. By noon, I had reached the stream I stopped at before and dismounted. I washed and dressed my wound again. The swelling and redness had subsided some, but the pain was still ferocious. I was feverish and getting delirious from the heat and pain. I passed through the hills and started across the bleak flat plain. By evening, I stopped at a small grove of desert willow, passed the night drifting in and out of delirium and got little rest.

Morning arrived hot and dry. A slight breeze had sprung up but made the heat more unbearable. I mounted my horse and set off. After riding for about two hours, drifting in and out of consciousness, and thought I saw riders coming toward me but kept plodding along.

"Easy fella," I heard a voice say as I fell unconscious again. I woke to find myself on a travois and surrounded by cavalry soldiers. They had thoughtfully rigged a shade to shield me from the burning sun. One of the soldiers noticed I was awake and shouted, "Lieutenant, he's awake."

The Lieutenant came over and said, "Dad! Thank God you are okay. We bandaged your wound; you did a good job of treating it yourself." I noticed my arm was in a sling and the pain had subsided considerably.

"Trent, is that you? Is Charlie Jr. with you?" I rasped.

"Yes," Trent said, and turning around yelled for Charlie.

Charlie Jr. came running over and said, "You had us worried for a while." He offered his canteen, and took a long draw before I spoke.

"How did you know I was out here?"

"I was dispatched to locate a Comanche raiding party seen in the area. I went into town to look you up and tell you. Louise told us you were out here chasing Roy for robbing the bank and murder. I wired the fort and Charlie Jr. was sent out with his detachment to locate you. We met up yesterday."

"I met up with them four days ago beyond the hills. Brave Eagle was leading them. After I spoke with them, they headed south."

"Is that Roy's horse?" asked Charlie Jr.

"Yes, the money he stole is in the saddlebags. He is beyond the plain in the narrow pass. I was in no shape to bury him."

"We'll take care of that detail," said Trent.

The sun was getting low in the sky and Trent turned to the Sargent and said, "Take charge of the saddlebags and make camp here and we'll start at first light."

The Sargent went over to the horse and retrieved the saddlebag. In short order, they had a fire going and rabbits were stewing in the pot over the fire. The sun had deserted the cloudless sky, and the cool breeze that sprang up felt good. Light from the stars and the full moon lit the area with a pale eerie glow and the flickering fire cast dancing shadows on the men and surrounding ground.

Trent and Charlie Jr. shared a plate of stew with their dad and talked some more before retiring for the night.

Conclusion

My Bio

It's time to wrap this up with a brief biological sketch, an overview of the material and some closing comments. I was born John Virgil Spillman in the year of our Lord 1948. I grew up in a small steel working village of McDonald, Ohio. Yes, I'm a buckeye. It was certainly considered country, and the road if you could call it a road, was mostly gravel. There was a large cow pasture across the road from our house that held the neighbor's cows. Our property was surrounded on two sides by woods. And one side by an open field where a neighbor farmer, Mr. Richards, cultivated hay.

My dad, named John Leamon Spillman was born in Olive Hill, Kentucky. My mom was born in Mann, West Virginia and named Bonnie Vivian O'Neal. As families go, I have one older sister and five younger sisters. Although my parents never went to church, they made it imperative that we did. At the tender age of thirteen, I heeded the alter call and accepted Jesus as my saviour. My grandfather, named Samuel Spillman, was a Baptist minister and influenced my decision to some degree. My mom was considered a homemaker by today's standards. My dad was a laborer at a block plant making cement blocks in a neighboring town. After he became disabled, we moved from the country to the city of Niles. I was in the sixth grade.

After we had moved, I was blessed with two younger brothers, ending up with a family size of nine. After I graduated high school, I traveled a lot. I spent some time in California as a sailor, spent a decade back in Ohio. After two failed marriages and numerous failed romances, I was on the road again. I spent six years in Georgia. I then moved to Arlington, Virginia. After seven years I was on the move again, this time to Texas. I then moved to Northern Indiana, southern Illinois, Kentucky and finally ending up in New Market, Virginia. Still wandering around, I moved to Harrisonburg, Virginia and eventually ended up where I am now in Stanley, Virginia.

I came back to the Lord after a long period of absence, mostly on my part as the Scriptures say He never changes. Life kept getting in the way, and after a long dry spell, I finally returned. I would never have guessed that this would be a major turning point in my life. I rededicated my life to the Lord, and have not turned back. I have a good friend named Donald Hutchins for which I am eternally grateful for starting me back on the path to the Lord. There are, of course many others that have contributed and I would be remiss in not acknowledging their contribution.

This material is in somewhat chronological order. A lot of my writings have been lost over time, and the surviving material is preserved in this collection. The tapestry woven into the poems, songs and short stories tell a tale of their own.

In Closing

... and a book of remembrance was written
before him for them that feared the LORD, ...
Malachi 3:16 KJV

Dear readers, we are here but for a season. We come into this world, are here for a short time and then, like the flowers of the field and are gone like a wisp. However we may deem to perceive it, the all-knowing Creator gathers us to Him in His time like a bouquet of flowers.

Everyone has a story to tell however brief. In the telling, you will be encouraging and aiding others in their journey through life. You will also give them the encouragement to publish their own story.

I want to thank all the kind folks that inspired me and encouraged me to put this in print. A special thanks to Morgan Phenix and Donald Hutchins for their unwavering support and encouragement.

–John V Spillman

Printed in the United States
By Bookmasters